LINKEDIN: 101 WAYS TO ROCK YOUR PERSONAL BRAND

LINKEDIN: 101 WAYS TO ROCK YOUR PERSONAL BRAND

Grow your network and build your business!

Viveka von Rosen and Dayna Steele

Daily Success
THE BOOK SERIES

ISBN-13: 9781537105376
ISBN-10: 153710537X

Large quantity purchases of this book are available at a discount. DAILY SUCCESS LLC books may be ordered through booksellers or by contacting:

DAILY SUCCESS LLC
a division of JFA INC
957 NASA Parkway Suite 101
Houston TX 77058
books@daynasteele.com
(281) 738-3254

Printed in the United States of America
Publish date: October 2016

*To my Mom, who taught me the proper use
of grammar. To my Dad, who showed me the importance
of networking. And to Alan, who supports me every step of
the way.
Viveka*

*To Dad, who taught me the awesome power
of a strong network.
Dayna*

OTHER BOOKS BY VIVEKA VON ROSEN

LinkedIn Marketing: An Hour a Day

LinkedIn Security: Who's Watching You

21 Days to Success with LinkedIn: Business Social
Networking the Gnik Rowten Way

OTHER BOOKS BY DAYNA STEELE

Surviving Alzheimer's with Friends, Facebook, and a
Really Big Glass of Wine

Havana: 101 Ways to Rock Your World

In the Classroom: 101 Ways to Rock Your World

Welcome to College! 101 Ways to Rock Your World

On the Golf Course: 101 Ways to Rock Your World

101 Ways to Rock Your World: Everyday Activities for
Success Every Day

Rock to the Top: What I Learned about Success from the
World's Greatest Rock Stars

LINKEDIN: 101 WAYS TO ROCK YOUR PERSONAL BRAND

LinkedIn is a business-oriented social networking service. Founded on December 14, 2002 and launched on May 5, 2003, it is mainly used for professional networking.

- Wikipedia

CONTENTS

Technology is a double-edged sword. Just as sales people are moving into the future, buyers are already ahead of us.

- Koka Sexton, Social Marketing, LinkedIn

INTRODUCTION

by Koka Sexton

You are the CEO of Me Inc. This is the mantra that was given to me 10 years ago that changed my life. Branding, more specifically a personal brand, is one of the most important items in your career you need to nurture. It's no longer enough just to have a strong work ethic and have past co-workers and managers willing to say nice things about you when you change jobs. If you do not have a personal brand or even better, a professional brand, you are going to have a hard time skipping levels up the proverbial ladder.

Once an inside sales rep, I pounded the phone trying to build my pipeline. Living paycheck to paycheck. It wasn't working out too well for me. I knew I needed to change something, I didn't know what. All that changed when I realized I had to build my own brand in order for people to even pay attention.

Visibility creates opportunity and the more I leveraged LinkedIn, the more my professional brand grew. Social media is the ultimate equalizer for companies and the individuals in them. When I started being thoughtful about how I built my network, stopped talking about me and focused on adding value, my network responded by helping me become the global leader in the social selling space.

Personal branding starts with YOU and your ability to become an invaluable resource for your industry. LinkedIn is the best platform available for professionals trying to build their professional brand. Your profile is only one component. You need to be creative and use the platform in different ways to have an impact. Lucky for you, it's all outlined in this book.

Grow your network strategically, add value, and search out the opportunities that are going to allow you to climb the ladder as well as skip levels and build even greater opportunities. There are no shortcuts but there are smartcuts. Those smartcuts are outlined here as the processes needed to successfully gain visibility and leverage social networks like LinkedIn to gain the attention of your buyers.

From an inside sales rep to leading the social media team at LinkedIn and now running my own company, this success is directly attributed to sweat equity and the opportunities LinkedIn as a platform provided to me. I've seen countless other professionals excel in their careers by using social media and I believe you will find the same successes if you follow these 101 tips.

LinkedIn: 101 Ways to Rock Your Personal Brand is a playbook you should follow from tip to tip to build your own path to success. Viveka von Rosen and Dayna Steele have mapped out what you need to do to get ahead using the power of LinkedIn.

Koka Sexton is often called the Godfather of Social Selling, having mastered the art of leveraging social media for sales professionals. An expert in professional branding, brand awareness, and generating leads through social networks; Sexton started his career in sales and grew through the ranks at LinkedIn to become the head of social media. He is currently the Founder of Social Selling Labs, an agency helping companies bridge the gap between sales and marketing with social media.

Personal Branding is the practice of people marketing themselves and their careers as brands. While previous self-help management techniques were about self-improvement, the personal-branding concept suggests instead that success comes from self-packaging.

- Google

OPENING WORDS

by Viveka von Rosen

Reid Hoffman, co-founder and former CEO of LinkedIn says, "The fastest way to change yourself is to hang out with people who are already the way you want to be."

I met Dayna Steele in 2011 and decided I wanted to be her when I grew up. It took some time, but we have shared a stage, and now a book together. Why is this important? When you create your online persona, your personal brand, you have to start with the bigger picture in mind.

Have I always been an international Forbes recognized speaker? Um. No. Creating a powerful brand is a little bit business strategy and a little bit law of attraction. Create your brand on

LinkedIn and then work passionately to prove it true.

Over the years I have sold used cars (really), managed a business office (not well), and tried several other businesses (with success but not much interest). In 2006, I was introduced to the business social media platform LinkedIn at a networking event. It caught my attention and, finally, my passion. What I saw was an extremely useful business tool and a way to create a powerful personal brand. The more I learned about using LinkedIn, the more I wanted to share it with other professionals.

I saw LinkedIn was the perfect business tool for marketing and wrote the best seller, *LinkedIn Marketing: An Hour a Day*. Soon I was traveling the world to teach and talk about LinkedIn. As my value grew as a top social media influencer (*Forbes*, four years in a row), I realized LinkedIn was a powerful tool for personal branding.

Why does anyone need personal branding? You have to stand out from the crowd. A personal brand is how you appear to the world. *Succeed as Your Own Boss* author Melinda Emerson says, "Your personal brand is how other people see you online." And Jeff Bezos, founder and CEO of

Amazon says, "Your personal brand is what others say about you when you leave the room." You want to make sure you are starting with, and leaving behind, a good impression.

Tom Peters first wrote about personal branding in the 1997 article, "The Brand Called You."

> *Regardless of age, regardless of position, regardless of the business we happen to be in, all of us need to understand the importance of branding. We are CEOs of our own companies: Me Inc. To be in business today, our most important job is to be head marketer for the brand called You.*

You are your brand... whether you are an entrepreneur, jobseeker, or corporate employee, you can still define your brand within your business, no matter what that business is.

Koka Sexton (who wrote our introduction) was the Head of Social Media, Member Marketing & Communications at LinkedIn. He built his Social Selling brand within LinkedIn. So when he decided to leave LinkedIn (ironically during the writing of this book), his already established brand meant he was able to launch his Social Selling Labs business with a running and successful start.

LinkedIn gives you the ability to not only be seen by the world but control how the world sees you. With, at publish date, more than 450 million members in 200 countries and territories around the globe, LinkedIn gives you access to a network like never before. When utilized effectively, LinkedIn opens the door to people, jobs, news, updates, and insights that will increase your odds of success substantially.

The key phrase here, *when utilized effectively*, is why we wrote this book. LinkedIn is a powerful tool and a free one as well. Though there are paid services, most of what you can do for your own success with LinkedIn isn't going to cost you anything other than your own time and effort. And since we all know time is money, this book will help you best streamline your efforts and help you find all LinkedIn has to offer to grow your professional network.

A book does not write itself. To succeed, like anything, it needs a network. Thanks to Gold Level Hospitality speaker and consultant Colin Gold for taking the time to be our beta reader. I want to thank my team members at SocialSales GPS, Michael de Groot, Beth Granger, Mario Martinez Jr., Colleen McKenna, Ted Prodromou, Lindsey

Stemann, Brynne Tillman, and Bob Woods for always keeping me up to date and on my toes with all things LinkedIn.

You have a great service or product. Now, let's make sure those 450 million members in 200 countries can find you on LinkedIn and understand you are the best. There are 101 helpful tips in this book that will do just that.

Viveka von Rosen is an internationally known LinkedIn speaker and author. She has taken the business knowledge she has perfected over the past 10+ years and transformed it into engaging and informational training, providing over 100K+ people with the tools and strategies they need to succeed on LinkedIn.

YOUR BRAND

Today you are you. That is truer than true. There is no one alive who is youer than you!

- Dr. Suess, Author

1. GET FOCUSED

Who are you? What do you do? Who do you do it for? What do they get out of it? Answer these questions before you even get started. Take some time and talk to those who know you best – it's the best way to create clear answers.

2. BE CLEAR

Clarity is key to personal branding. The clearer you can be with your answers to the questions in the first tip, the better you will relay your skill-set to others. The clearer you are, the more likely you are to convert your prospects into customers.

3. BE MEMORABLE

If you can tell a prospect how they benefit from buying your service or product, you become memorable. Using a cosmetics salesperson's pitch as an example, which one would you buy from?

- I can help anyone with a face.
- I help 40+ women present themselves to the public in their best and most youthful light.

The foundation for any marketing – content or otherwise – is your target audiences, buyer personas, customer profiles, industry segments – whatever you want to call this directed and in-depth research and depiction of who buys what from you and why.

- Ardath Albee, Author and Speaker

4. WRITE A CLIENT DESCRIPTION

This isn't something you'll ever really post on LinkedIn, but it helps establish who you are talking to in your own mind. Create a *buyer persona* of your typical client or customer – age, sex, job, what they use you or your product for, etc. Imagining someone in your mind helps when it comes time to build a strong LinkedIn profile. Know your audience.

5. CREATE YOUR OWN KEYWORDS

When you create your list of keywords, think about the search terms people would use when Googling someone like you. Titles, industries, companies, names, locations, skills, products, and services are all keywords. Think verb, noun, acronym and synonym: accountant, CPA, accounting, book-keeping, Quickbooks.

6. HAVE A GOOD ELEVATOR SPEECH

Who are you, and what makes you different from the other person who does what you do for the same clients? Figure out what that is and learn to say it in one compelling sentence. Elevators are fast these days. Knowing how to do this is an important key to successful branding and to writing a good professional headline.

Summary

I am a passionate entrepreneur and master of social media for business. As the author of the #1 selling eBook Instagram Basics for Your Business, I am a sought-after speaker who has presented at events including the acclaimed Social Media Marketing World as well as the Social Media Camp, the largest conference of its kind in Canada. Her expertise in visual content marketing has been featured on CreativeLive. Retail store owner of SueBDo, I also lend my expertise to coaching and training companies to leverage the power of social media platforms.

With my extensive knowledge of social media, my ease and comfort with people, and my creative eye for branding, I am a master at connecting and empowering others to be successful entrepreneurs and marketing gurus. I've found a really awesome niche teaching social media to clients and absolutely love the power of Instagram. It has helped me build my own network and increase sales and I am inspired to teach others what I know.

7. YOUR ONE PARAGRAPH PITCH

Once you have gotten someone's attention with your elevator speech, be able to elaborate even more by filling in a few more details but still answering the questions; who are you, what do you do, who do you it for, and what do they get out of it? Three to five sentences for this paragraph is a good length.

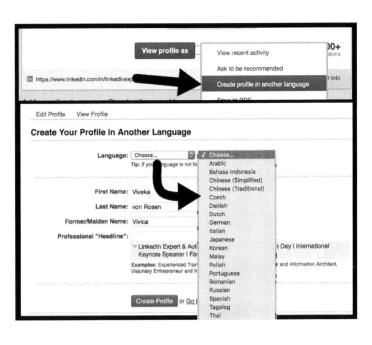

8. WHAT LANGUAGES DO YOUR CLIENTS AND YOU SPEAK?

Linkedin allows you to have your profile in many different languages. If you serve an international clientele anywhere in the world, create a profile in English as well as in the language of the clients you serve and the languages you speak. A definite plus to any profile.

The language, especially the vocabulary, peculiar to a particular trade, profession, or group: such as medical jargon.

- Dictionary.com

9. WHAT JARGON DO YOUR CLIENTS REGULARLY USE?

Marketing or sales prospects will expect to see words like ROI and KPI. The average person might not know what that means, but your ideal client knows what it is. Add relevant jargon to your keyword list and sprinkle those into various sections of your profile.

10. BE CONSISTENT IN ALL YOUR BRANDING

Once you are clear on who you are, what you do and whom you serve, create relevant and consistent written copy, visuals, and shared content everywhere on LinkedIn – including your profile picture. If you claim to be a serious businessperson, don't share silly cat videos in your feed. You get the idea.

PROFILE OPTIMIZATION

You develop your LinkedIn profile in a few hours. You develop your personal brand over time, and it's your opportunity to share your work, values, passion, and personality with the world.

- Colleen McKenna, Social Selling Expert

11. YOUR NAME

Take a minute to check you have your correct name on LinkedIn. Double-check your spelling. Unless you are ee cummings, capitalize your name.

You never get a second chance to make a great first impression and your LinkedIn profile is your chance to make a great first professional impression.

- Ted Prodromou, LinkedIn Author and Speaker

12. USE YOUR NAME AND ONLY YOUR NAME ON LINKEDIN

You might see some people use their area of expertise in the last name field, such as "John Doe: Master of the Universe." This is against LinkedIn's User Agreement. Don't add your area of expertise, telephone number, email address, or your call to action in the Name field. If LinkedIn catches you doing this, they will make your profile unfindable in Search.

Colin Gold

Distinguish your Business! Create a Client Experience
Culture. Keynote Speaker, Facilitator, Consultant

Miami/Fort Lauderdale Area | Professional Training & Coaching

Current	Gold Level Hospitality and Consulting
Previous	KW PROPERTY MANAGEMENT AND CONSULTING, The James Hotel New York, Trump International Beach Resort
Education	University of Massachusetts, Amherst

Send a message ▼

500+
connections

13. CUSTOMIZE YOUR PROFESSIONAL HEADLINE

The section right under your name is your professional headline. Take a look at the branding you created from the first few tips in this book. You have 120 characters to describe who you are, what you do, and whom you serve. Try to utilize some of the keywords you have created in this section.

14. CREATE YOUR CONTENT
IN WORD FIRST

A good rule of thumb when creating content for LinkedIn (or really for anything), is to write it in Word or Pages first, and then check your spelling and grammar. Nothing says non-professional like misspellings and bad grammar. Plus, if you do it in Word first, you can count characters, and maximize the space you have to brand yourself.

15. FILL IN YOUR SUMMARY SECTION

You have 2000 characters to describe in detail who you are, what you do, and whom you serve in the very important Summary section. Start with the one paragraph pitch you've already written. Then, use the buyer persona and the keywords you've created to pitch to that perfect customer in your Summary section. For a professional and visually pleasing summary, use white space, special characters, bullets, and capitalization.

Develop a standard for excellence. Without distinction, there is extinction.

- Jon Michal, CEO Image International

16. WHAT'S IN IT FOR THEM?

Social sales, social marketing, and social branding – all key elements of LinkedIn - are all about the same end result. What's in it for the customer? If you can speak their language, fill their needs, and assuage their fears - you'll find yourself and your brand to be more successful in LinkedIn. Think about this as you create any content on your profile.

17. ARE YOU EXPERIENCED?

The Experience section on your profile is where you get to talk about you and your company. You have 2000 characters to describe your company, what your company does, and what you do for the company. You can list services, features, and unique selling propositions here. Always highlight what makes you and your company different from everyone else.

18. ADD YOUR EDUCATION

Whether you have your MBA from Harvard or a degree in the "Hard Knocks of Life," add your education to LinkedIn. It is part of who you are. You have 1000 characters to describe what you did in school and why it's relevant to who you are today. Even if what you studied is totally different from where you are today, add it. It adds to your character.

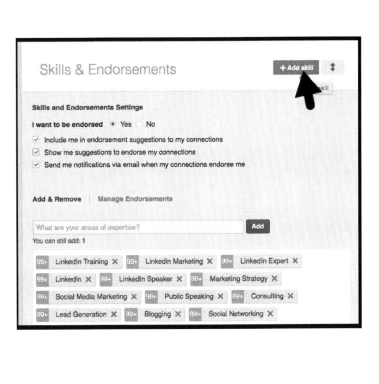

19. LIST YOUR SKILLS

You can add up to 50 skills in this section on your profile. Add as many as you can. Choose the skills *you* want to highlight, otherwise LinkedIn might suggest skills you don't actually have. List your skills in the order you think is important, not the default (which is chronological). The first 10 skills listed will get the most endorsements.

It's important to build a personal brand because it's the only thing you're going to have. Your reputation online and in the business world is pretty much the same, so be a good person. You can't hide anything, and more importantly, you've got to be out there at some level.

- Gary Vaynerchuck, Influencer

20. BECOME MORE FINDABLE

You want people to be able to find you by the keywords and skills associated with your brand. The more skill endorsements you have, the more findable you are on LinkedIn. The more you are known for something, the more likely it is you will be endorsed for it, and the more findable you become. To get more endorsements actively endorse others. And make sure you have your setting on to give and get endorsements.

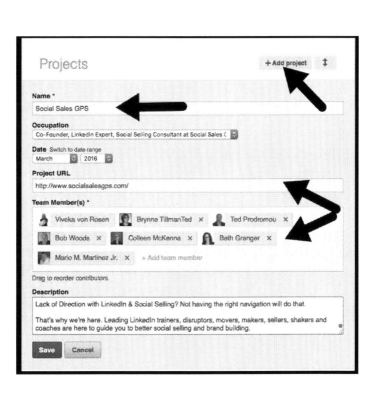

21. ADD YOUR PROJECTS

If you are a contract laborer or consultant, the Projects section allows you to share details about the work you do without listing each and every one of the hundreds of jobs you've done in Experience. Just hit the highlights. If you are new to Projects, click on LinkedIn's Building Blocks called "Add a Section." If you've already added a project, just scroll down to that section and click on "Add Projects."

Publications

LinkedIn: 101 Ways to Rock Your World

HippoPress

2016

Create a strong personal brand to grow your network and build your business!

2 authors

 Viveka von Rosen
LinkedIn Expert & Author: LinkedIn Mark...

 Dayna Steele
Rockstar Storyteller, Speaker, Success A...

LinkedIn Marketing: An Hour a Day

John Wiley & Sons, Sybex Division

2012

This book will not only share LinkedIn features, but benefits and Best Practices from A-Z.

Whether a beginner at LinkedIn, or an advanced user, this book will not only fully outline everything a business person (including entrepreneurs, job seekers, B2B ad B2C) needs to fully comprehend the many differing aspects of LinkedIn (from Ad Creation to Zipcode Searches and everything in...

The Sophisticated Marketer's Guide to LinkedIn

LinkedIn

February 2014

The sophisticated marketer is someone who takes marketing techniques, both old and new, and executes them in an overall integrated marketing strategy.

This type of marketer is grounded in timeless, Mad Men-era tactics and combines them with new, modern
technology. What worked during the golden age of marketing still works today, but marketers need to adapt.

Social media...

▸ 10 authors, including:

 Viveka von Rosen
LinkedIn Expert & Author: LinkedIn Mark...

 Jason Miller

22. ADD AVAILABLE PUBLICATIONS

Not everyone is a published author, but you may be a content creator of some sort. If you write a blog, a newsletter, an eBook, or use LinkedIn Publisher, you are now considered a Publisher by LinkedIn. You don't want to list every blog post you have ever created, but do choose a few which really support your brand.

LinkedIn is your own personal, yet professional brand online. Creating your brand can be easy. You need to do it in a quality way that both promotes the value you bring to those people visiting your LinkedIn Profile, and attracts the people who you are seeking in your branding efforts.

- Bob Woods, LinkedIn Expert and Co-Founder of Social Sales GPS

23. ADD YOUR ORGANIZATIONS AND VOLUNTEER WORK

Organizations you belong to and volunteer work you do both lend an emotional quality to your brand that helps to increase positive brand sentiment. Do consider leaving political and religious organizations out of this section - unless that IS your brand. Remember the Dayna Steele rule: Stay away from politics, religion, and cats – you'll always alienate half your audience if you don't.

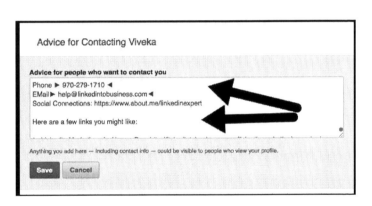

Advice for Contacting Viveka

Advice for people who want to contact you

Phone ▶ 970-279-1710 ◀
EMail▶ help@linkedintobusiness.com ◀
Social Connections: https://www.about.me/linkedinexpert

Here are a few links you might like:

Anything you add here — including contact info — could be visible to people who view your profile.

Save   Cancel

24. ADD YOUR CONTACT INFORMATION

You can have the best brand in the world, but if you don't give people a way to contact you, it may not do you much good. Add your email address in the Contact section. If you add a phone number, your private cell number may not be a good idea. This section is public on LinkedIn.

25. CUSTOMIZE YOUR URL

Your public profile should reflect your name, your business, or your area of expertise. On the Edit Profile page, go to the edit icon to the right of the URL under your headshot. In the page that opens, add your personal branding to the URL there on the right side of the page. Don't use any special characters or spaces.

26. CUSTOMIZE YOUR WEBSITE LINKS

O n the Edit Profile page, click on Contact Info (under your number of connections). Scroll down beneath your email address and phone number and click on the websites box. When you edit your website, the drop down menu gives you the option of "other." When you click on that, a new field opens up to allow you to type in a new title such as "Click here for more info."

VISUALS AND MEDIA

Post with visuals drive up to 180% more engagement than those without.

- Ekaterina Walter, Author, Speaker, and Influencer

27. ADD BRANDING GRAPHICS

LinkedIn is becoming more visual. Pictures sell. If you are not a graphic artist, then invest in a graphic artist; use the freelancers at Fiverr.com or any number of tools and sites online to help you create better graphics. The more visually professional your profile looks, the better you look.

28. USE A HEADER IMAGE

Upload a header or background image on your personal profile (current LinkedIn size is 1400x425 and is subject to change). This is one of the easiest ways to emphasize your personal brand on LinkedIn. For example, if you work for a company or represent a product, incorporate (with permission) the branding including colors, fonts, logos, workplace photos, etc. into your header image and contact information.

Dayna Steele

Rockstar Storyteller, Speaker, S
Alzheimer's Fighter, Caring.com
Broadway Investor

Houston, Texas Area | Professional Tr

Current	Speaker Dayna Steele, Da
	Entertainment & Theatrical
Previous	Your Daily Success Tip, Th
Education	Texas A&M University

View profile as ▾

29. ADD A PROFESSIONAL PROFILE PHOTO

This is not the place for a logo or your latest vacation photo. Use a photo that looks like someone your customers would want to do business with. How do you present yourself in front of customers in person? That's what you want here – a current, professional looking headshot or a good shot of you in action doing what it is you do.

Your profile picture validates who you are and supports the narrative that you are likeable, competent, and trustworthy.

- Guy Kawasaki, Author and Social Media Evangelist

30. THIS CENTURY PLEASE

The word "current" bears repeating here. When uploading your image, your headshot needs to look enough like you, so when you go to a conference, a trade show, or a job interview, you won't get blank stares due to a complete lack of recognition.

Googling yourself is not vain. It is a necessary tactic for managing your personal identity.

- Maya Demishkevich, Author

31. GOOGLE YOURSELF

Search your name, product, service – whatever your brand is – online. There may be videos or other media you can share. Keep those that are business or brand related. It is also a good way to find out if there is anything negative about you or your product or service online. Fix that ASAP.

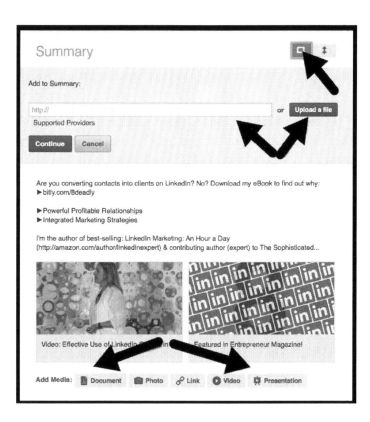

Summary

Add to Summary:

http://   or   Upload a file

Supported Providers

Continue   Cancel

Are you converting contacts into clients on LinkedIn? No? Download my eBook to find out why:
▶ bitly.com/8deadly

▶ Powerful Profitable Relationships
▶ Integrated Marketing Strategies

I'm the author of best-selling: LinkedIn Marketing: An Hour a Day
(http://amazon.com/author/linkedinexpert) & contributing author (expert) to The Sophisticated...

Video: Effective Use of LinkedIn   Featured in Entrepreneur Magazine!

Add Media: 📄 Document   📷 Photo   🔗 Link   ▶ Video   🎨 Presentation

32. UPLOAD YOUR TALENT

PowerPoint presentations, Word documents, PDFs, and other media show your expertise and support your personal brand. LinkedIn gives you an Add Media option to upload these items. If you have already added media, there is a media icon with a plus sign that, once clicked, will allow you to upload additional media or add a link. Audit your computer files to see what you might could use.

33. ADD VIDEO LINKS

Just as graphics and photos are important to your profile, so is video. Video showcases your personality, your product, your service, and your admirers. Interviews, product demos, and testimonials add so much more to your profile – building credibility and showcasing your expertise. This is a good space to add any positive television coverage you may have received. Add video as a YouTube or Vimeo link.

34. UTILIZE SLIDESHARE

Do you have a portfolio or a killer PowerPoint presentation? Create or recreate it in Slideshare. There are some amazing resumes transcribed to multi-media events using Slideshare. When you add a PowerPoint presentation, LinkedIn will convert it to Slideshare if you have an account. (Slideshare is free.) That creates get more visibility for your brand.

35. ADD MORE PICTURES

In addition to your professional headshot, add other photographs that brand you and your work. You can upload a picture of a project you have completed, an award you have won, a certificate you have received, or fascinating people you met at a conference. Again, remember to keep those images professional. This is not the place to highlight your recent vacation.

36. ADD ADDITIONAL PDFS

Does your company have a brochure? Upload the PDF. Do you have a resume or a great cover letter? How about a chapter of your book? Take a section and upload it as a PDF. A word of advice - remove any personal contact information from your resume before you add the PDF.

37. A WORD ABOUT WORD

Word documents are great but always be careful with which ones you upload - anyone can download a Word document and make it their own.

CREATING
CREDIBILITY

Recommendations

Ask to be recommended Manage

Founder, Professional LinkedIn Strategist, Keynote Speaker, LinkedIn & Social Media Expert
Linked Into Business

Dayna Steele
Story Teller | Keynote Speaker | Success Author and Strategist | Alzheimer's Fighter and Caring.com Chief Caring Expert

" I had the opportunity to interview Viveka at a conference several years ago and then see one of her presentations. I was so impressed (and learned so much), I decided to keep her as a good friend as well as a business associate. See the video here: https://youtu.be/rrdTVRStl20. We are currently collaborating on a book - LinkedIn: 101 Ways to Rock Your Personal Branding... **more** "

May 27, 2016, Dayna was with another company when working with Viveka at Linked Into Business

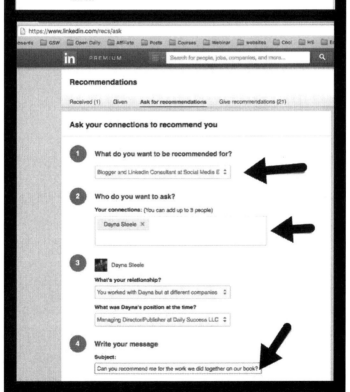

38. YOU MUST BE CONNECTED
FOR A RECOMMENDATION

If there is someone you want a recommendation from – or you would like to recommend – you need to first be connected on LinkedIn. Send a connection request. If you want to recommend this person, let them know that as well. Don't ask right away for a recommendation; let this person connect with you first. Consider it business foreplay.

Recommendations

Keynote Speaker, Corporate Emcee, Live Interviews or
Speaker Dayna Steele

Debi Kensell
Education Director - Restaurant Facility Management Association (F

" Dayna Steele is an amazing speaker and wonderful to work with
for two separate events and received rave reviews! Thanks Dayna f
great partner at our RFMA 2016 annual conference in Nashville and
Association Day in Dallas! You definitely make us all look like Rock:

June 28, 2016, Debi was Dayna's client

Sarah Stealey Reed
Director of Content Marketing at Zendesk

" Dayna is a gift. She's naturally a dynamic and engaging speaker
importantly—she is human. And her human qualities of genuinenes
authenticity shine through with every presentation and talk. Dayna v
that resonates with the audience, while providing meaningful execu
every interaction with a room full of excited and... **more** "

June 9, 2016, Sarah was with another company when working with Dayn
Steele

Viveka von Rosen
LinkedIn Expert & Author: LinkedIn Marketing Hour a Day I Internati
Speaker I Forbes Top 20 Most Influential

" Dayna is ... I can't even begin to describe how awesome she is. I
one of the coolest careers in the history of music (and marketing) a

39. GET STARTED WITH RECOMMENDATIONS

Nothing is better than others talking about how great you are. LinkedIn has a feature that allows you to ask for and give recommendations. Unless you already have recommendations, the ask link is hard to find – use www.linkedin.com/recs/ask. If you do already have recommendations, you will find an Ask for Recommendations and Manage link in the Recommendations section of your profile.

40. HOW TO ASK FOR A RECOMMENDATION

Do not use LinkedIn's default copy when asking for a recommendation. In the Subject field, remind people how they know you. In the body, ask for the recommendation by reminding them what you did together and how well it went. Always end with appreciation.

41. COMPOSE YOUR OWN RECOMMENDATION

People are busy and will often ignore a request for a recommendation. Don't take it personally. In your ask, add a sample of what you are looking for and say, "If this looks good to you, feel free to copy and paste into the recommendation." More often than not, people will say 'that looks fine' and will use it to recommend you.

42. RECOMMEND OTHERS

If you are not getting the recommendations you are asking for, then try recommending others on LinkedIn. Perhaps a nice recommendation will inspire them to recommend you. Never, ever ask or write recommendations for people you don't know or haven't worked with.

43. USING A TESTIMONIAL FROM ELSEWHERE

If you have a testimonial from someone, but you are not connected to that person on LinkedIn, find their profile and invite them to connect. Once connected, follow up with a message asking to use the testimonial as a recommendation. Copy and paste the whole testimonial and give them the link to recommend you: https://www.linkedin.com/recs/give.

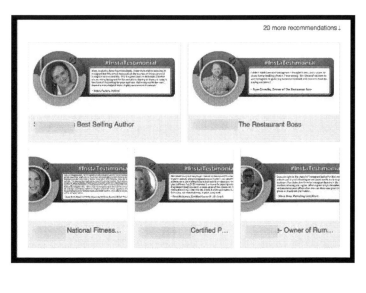

44. REPURPOSING OLD TESTIMONIALS

If you have a stellar testimonial, but the author is not on LinkedIn (or won't connect to you) then you can always upload the testimonial as an image, as a PDF or even put a bunch of testimonials together in a Slideshare presentation. You can even copy and paste shortened testimonials right into the "Description" sections of your Summary, Experience, and Education.

In a world of endless spin, scandals, and something-gates, what people are really after is authenticity. They want to know what your goods or services are really like. Anything that smacks of corporate spin will backfire, writing off your testimonials as worthless or, worse yet, dishonest. The effectiveness of your testimonials is tied to how authentic users believe them to be.

- RocketSpark.com

45. VISUAL TESTIMONIALS

If a picture is worth a thousand words, imagine what a video testimonial is worth. It is too easy to shoot quality video these days with your phone – so no excuses. Get some video testimonials, upload them to YouTube or another video site, and add them to your profile.

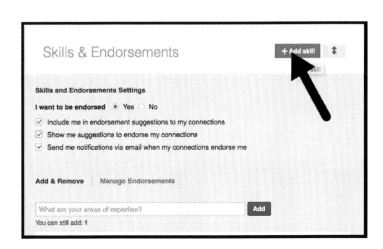

46. GET ENDORSEMENTS

Endorsements are really more of a Facebook "like" than a true testimonial to your awesomeness, but they still count. Make sure your Skills list is up-to-date, then endorse a few of your friends for their skills. Is your endorsement feature turned on? Remember, these endorsements make you more easily found on LinkedIn.

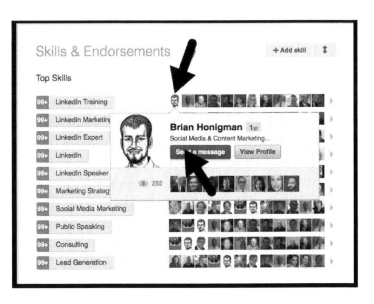

47. THANK YOUR ENDORSERS

When someone endorses you, LinkedIn will send you an email where you can return the favor and say thanks. Go to your Skills section and scroll over their picture - you will be able to send them a quick thank you. Ask them what skills they would like endorsed. Start a conversation. Build rapport. Make a new friend and maybe even a new client. Success is a reciprocal thing.

A brand is simply trust.

- Steve Jobs, Apple

48. LIST OF YOUR ENDORSEMENTS

When you go into Settings, (in the dropdown menu on the top right of your profile,) in the Basics section (default) click on Get an Archive of Your Data. LinkedIn will send you an Excel file with your endorsements. Now you can use the sort feature to see which of your Connections endorsed you the most. These are relationships you should nurture.

The fastest way to change yourself is to hang out with people who are already the way you want to be.

- Reid Hoffman, Founder of LinkedIn

YOUR BEST
PROSPECTS

The aim of marketing is to know and understand the customer so well the product or service fits him (or her) and sells itself.

- Peter Drucker, Author and Management Consultant

49. SEARCH FOR YOUR PERFECT CUSTOMER

Even if you are not in sales or marketing, you need the buyer persona you created earlier. The keywords, titles, and industries from that persona are a good place to start. LinkedIn won't let you search your network by economic qualifications, sex, or age. You can search by title, company, industry, keyword, name, school, and a variety of other free search fields.

Good marketers see consumers as complete human beings with all the dimensions real people have.

- Jonah Sachs, Author

50. USING ADVANCED SEARCH FOR CONNECTIONS

The more refined a search, the better. You might get less people in the search results, but they will be of higher quality and better potential to you. The Advanced Search feature is best for finding these personas to connect with. Click on the Advanced Search link and start filling in the fields to find your targeted prospects.

51. OTHER PROSPECT ADVANCED SEARCH CRITERIA

While starting with your own keywords and customer profile is best, LinkedIn's Advanced Search will allow you to search by:

- Profile keywords like entrepreneur or artistic
- Titles such as HR, Consultant, Job-seeker, Guru
- Companies where key connections might work
- Schools your prospects have attended
- Postal Codes where your connections live

52. USE THE BOOLEAN SEARCH METHOD

A t this time, free members only get to see 100 search results (and sometimes less.) Using the Boolean qualifiers (AND, OR, NOT) will better sort your search results, organizing them in a logical way and more usable form as well as excluding those who don't meet your criteria for a prospect. Keep reading for usage tips and examples…

53. THE POWER OF OR

People use different words to describe themselves or their skills in their profiles. A business owner might call herself CEO, Managing Director, President, Founder, or Partner. Use a capitalized OR to include different titles for this search method such as CEO OR "Chief Executive Officer" OR Owner OR President. Quotation marks are used to hold words together in a search.

54. THE POWER OF AND

The use of AND refines your search when you want a specific term included in the search. Example: CEO OR "Chief Executive Officer" OR Founder OR Owner OR President AND beer AND microbrewery. AND is capitalized for this type of search.

55. NOT GETS RID OF ALL
THE RIFF RAFF

As you have probably figured out, NOT excludes people from your search. Example: CEO OR "Chief Executive Officer" OR Founder OR Owner OR President AND beer AND microbrewery NOT LinkedIn Expert NOT spammers NOT tomatoes. Capitalize NOT.

56. CREATE YOUR SEARCH IN A WORD DOCUMENT

Create your search in a Word document. This catches spelling errors and allows you to see the whole search string. It makes changing the search much easier. Once you like your search words, pop the new string into the appropriate field and adjust as needed. This usually includes adding more NOTs.

57. ZERO DOESN'T ALWAYS MEAN ZERO

If you get zero search results, there is likely a spelling error in your search. The first step is to make sure there are no errors by checking your Word doc (or use Grammarly.com). If there are no errors, then sign out of LinkedIn and sign back in. Sometimes LinkedIn acts up. If you still get no results, try different search terms or expand your search.

Marketing OR technology OR healthcare OR CPG OR "consumer packaged goods" OR fashion OR footwear OR hospitality OR tourism OR "food beverage" NOT opportunities NOT secretary NOT assistant NOT consultant NOT LinkedIn NOT copywriter NOT recruiter NOT experienced NOT communications NOT consultant

VP+Marketing OR vice+marketing OR CMO OR Chief+Marketing OR marketing+Director OR director+marketing

https://www.linkedin.com/vsearch/p?keywords=Marketing%20OR%20technology%20OR%20healthcare%20OR%20CPG%20OR%20%E2%80%9Cconsumer%20packaged%20goods%E2%80%9D%20OR%20fashion%20OR%20footwear%20OR%20hospitality%20OR%20tourism%20OR%20%E2%80%9Cfood%20beverage%E2%80%9D%20NOT%20opportunities%20NOT%20secretary%20NOT%20assistant%20NOT%20consultant%20NOT%20LinkedIn%20NOT%20copywriter%20NOT%20recruiter%20NOT%20experienced%20NOT%20Communications&title=VP%2BMarketing%20OR%20vice%2Bmarketing%20OR%20CMO%20OR%20Chief%2BMarketing%20OR%20marketing%2BDirector%20OR%20director%2Bmarketing&openAdvancedForm=true&titleScope=C&locationType=I&countryCode=us&f_G=us%3A84,us%3A49,us%3A732,us%3A51,us%3A748&f_CS=3,4,5,6,7,8&rsid=118415211467996098154&orig=FCTD&pt=people&f_N=F,S,A

58. SAVE THE SEARCH URLS

You have already created your search in a Word (or Pages) doc, now you want to save the search URL to the same document. Just copy it from the browser and paste it into your document. This allows you to easily populate the search or share it with your employees or colleagues. If you create a perfect prospect search and send that URL to your employees, they can refine it via location, industry, etc.

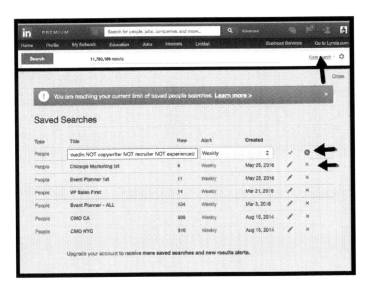

59. SAVE YOUR SEARCH RIGHT ON LINKEDIN

You can save three searches with a free LinkedIn account and more with a Premium account. Click on the Saved link on the top right side of your search - name and save the search. LinkedIn will send you a weekly digest of new people who fall into that particular search algorithm. Keep in mind; unless you make yourself anonymous in settings, your prospects will see when you have viewed their profiles.

60. SEARCHING FOR ALUMNI

Click on the dropdown next to the main search box at the top of your profile. Click on Universities in the dropdown menu and type your university or college name in the search box. Click on your institution of higher learning. When your school's page opens, click on the Students and Alumni link. You can also click on Find Alumni under My Network.

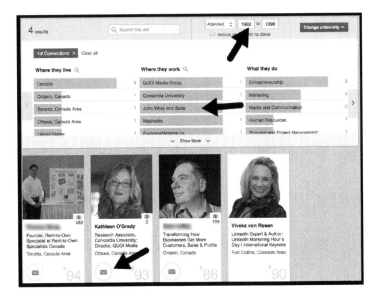

61. CONNECTING WITH ALUMNI

Going to the same school creates an initial connection. Search alumni according to when they went to school, where they work, where they live, what they do, what they studied, what they are skilled at, and even how you are connected. Send a message to first level connections and send an invite to second level connections.

62. SEARCHING COMPANIES

Search companies you would like to do business with. Click on the Companies page option in the top Smart Search dropdown box. Type in the name of the Company you are interested in. If the company has a page, you will see How You're Connected on the right of the Company Page. LinkedIn will sort employees for you so you can send a message to first level connections and invite other levels to connect.

My Groups   Discover

Sales Best Practices
290,862 members

Sales Best Practices
290,862 members

MEMBERS LIST

Members Pending Admins

🔍 CEO OR Founder

Mark Hartsell, MBA, CEO
CEO Advisor, Inc.

Colleen Stanley, CEO
SalesLeadership Inc. Sales Keynote Speaker, Emotional Intelligence For Sales Su...

Lisa Peskin, CEO
Sales and Sales Management Consulting, Training & Coaching | Sales Force Analy...

63. SEARCHING GROUPS

Groups are good sources because technically you already share something in common with other group members. Once you have joined a group, click on the number of members. Don't click on the blue Member link because then you will leave the group. Once you have clicked on the number of members, you can do a search for a member by name or title.

64. SEARCHING YOUR CONNECTIONS' CONNECTIONS

Find someone you know on LinkedIn and click on the *blue* number of connections in their Bio section. If the number is black, your connection has this service blocked. The link will take you into their connections section. Click on the magnifying glass icon to expand it into a search box. Now all you have to do is search on a keyword or title to see who they know.

65. INVITING CONNECTION'S CONNECTIONS

When you find someone in a search you want to connect with, you can invite him or her to connect very easily. Click on the Connect button and introduce yourself as in: Hello (name here), I see what we share (your mutual connection) in common. I would like to add you as a connection in my network.

66. SENDING A CUSTOMIZED INVITATION

Even though it's hard to see personalized invitations on the LinkedIn website with its current configuration, you can easily see them on the LinkedIn mobile app. Customize your invitation to those you want to connect with. Even though you are limited to 300 characters, add as much of your voice and personality as you can to the invitation.

If people like you they will listen to you. But if they trust you, they'll do business with you.

- Zig Ziglar, Author and award-winning Salesman

67. BE CONSERVATIVE ABOUT WHO YOU REACH OUT TO

Don't go crazy and invite everyone to join your network. You are limited to 3000 invitations and while LinkedIn might give you more if you ask, they could look at your history and refuse you if you have too many people who have said they don't know you - known as an IDK. This is yet another reason why sending a customized invite is so important.

68. ASKING FOR AN INTRODUCTION

At this writing, LinkedIn's Introduction tool is a bit of a mess. Sometimes, emailing or phoning your shared contact is the best way to ask for an introduction. However, if you are not really comfortable asking for the introduction in real life, then take a chance and use the Introduction link on your prospect's profile.

Being introduced invites you into the conversation and makes you feel like part of the group. Making introductions is particularly important in business settings as they establish a rapport of respect, get relationships off on the right foot, and give you an aura of being confident, prepared, and in control.

- Bret and Kate McKay, The Art of Manliness

69. TAGGING YOUR CONNECTIONS

Tagging is very similar to Facebook or Twitter lists in it allows you to segment and manage your connections in a way that makes sense to you. At this time, you can tag your 1st level connection from their profile by clicking on the relationship tab under their name. Or you can go to My Connections and tag some or all of your connections in one go.

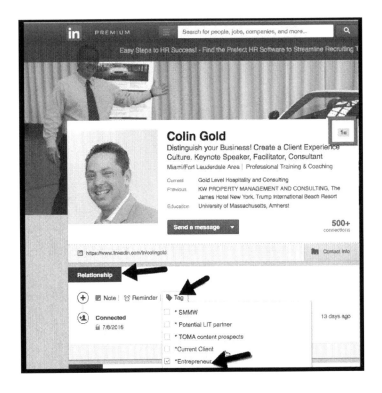

70. TAGS ARE YOUR SECRET

Your connections cannot see how you tag them. You can tag your connections in whatever manner you need when creating a strategy to keep engaged. Example: Hot Prospect, New Client San Francisco, Best Client, etc.

71. GETTING YOUR MESSAGE ACROSS

You have the opportunity to share private messages on LinkedIn. It's one of the best ways for you to develop relationships and your brand through personal engagement. This is never a good place to send a group message – use Messenger for individual private messages.

If your stories are all about your products and services, that's not storytelling. It's a brochure. Give yourself permission to make the story bigger.

- Jay Baer, Author, Speaker, and Influencer

72. MESSAGING VIA THE 80/20 RULE

Unless your brand is being a spammy spambot, then only use LinkedIn Messenger to share information and content your prospects and clients would be interested in. Don't spam your connections with your free webinar or pitch for your new product. After a few messages back and forth, you can ask for a phone call or a meeting.

What NOT to do in an InMail

Bonnie teater
To: Viveka von Rosen, LinkedIn Speaker <linkedinvv@gmail.com>
Reply-To: Bonnie teater (via LinkedIn)
asking permission/I do not want to break rules or offend anyone

LinkedIn

From: [ ] teater ← **Many spam accounts have last names that are not capitalized**
Date: 5/04/2014
Subject: asking permission/I do not want to break rules or offend anyone

Dear Viveka Van Rosen:

Spell my name correctly if you are going to ask me for money!

I have been a member for several years. I never thought I would need help, even though I am disabled from strokes, seizures, nerve damage in my neck, a fractured displaced tail bone and several other medical problems.

I became a funeral director because my parents needed help and I was the only one willing. I never got a paycheck, my parents wanted me to have the business. My father died in 2008 and my mother died in 2013. That is when my sisters decided they owned the business and they are going to sell it, I've got it going, without pay because it is my parents legacy and because I promised my parents [ ] that is best for everyone.

This has all the grammatical markers of a Sweetheart Scam.

On December 30, 2013, my car blew up in my garage and burnt up app. 70% of my home and everything in it, I have insurance, but it is not covering the car and everything is being depreciated. The insurance company is not renewing home policies, so on May 30, my family and I will have no home and no insurance because the house won't be done and I will not get any of the depreciated value on the repairs and I will need to be able to pay $15,000 to the contractors, pay taxes and my mortgage is due every month. Ive managed to budget $720 a month and take care of everything, but it is too much now.

I want to know if I can ask for $0.10 from all the members to help me get back on my feet. I know this is an unusual request, but I am in an unusual situation. Ten cents is no big deal to most people but it would make a huge difference in and my kids life, but a lot of dimes will make a huge difference in my life.

You want ME to set up a donation program for you?

If it is possible to set up a donation program for me and my family, to help us recover and to help me financially support my family, as soon as my seizures allow, it would be greatly appreciated. Please consider my request and let me know if it is at all possible. Thank you. Bonnie GT Brookshier

Is your name Bonnie Brookshier or Bonnie teater. I'm so confused.

View/reply to this message

when copying and pasting check that you don't have two stories mixed in together

Don't want to receive e-mail notifications? Adjust your message settings

This email was intended for Viveka von Rosen (LinkedIn Expert & Author, LinkedIn Marketing Hour a Day, International Keynote Speaker | Forbes Top 20 Most Influential. Learn why we included this. © 2014, LinkedIn Corporation, 2029 Stierlin Ct. Mountain View, CA 94043, USA

73. PROPER USE OF INMAIL

nMails are paid messages you can use to send private messages to people who are NOT your first level connections. They can be very effective when used to get to know someone. They are not at all effective if you are blasting a bunch of sales messages or recruiting messages to people who neither know, like, nor trust you yet. InMail will cost you $10 a pop if you have the free account. Use these only as a last result.

I've learned that people will forget what you said, people will forget what you did, but people will never forget how you made them feel.

- Maya Angelou, Author and Poet

CONTENT MARKETING

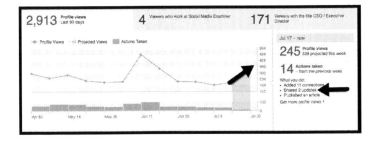

74. SHARE MORE UPDATES

Sharing even one update a week will increase the visibility of your profile. Once a day is even better. Your profile is your brand; so increased visibility will increase your prospects' sense of knowing, liking, and trusting you, which leads to increased business. Share something you read or create your own content. Keep it professional and relevant to your business and brand.

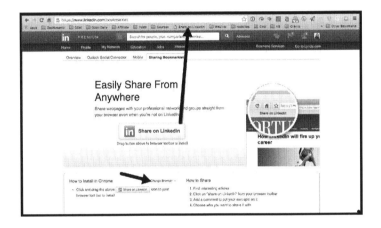

75. USE THE SHARING BOOKMARKLET

You don't have to use a paid social media scheduler to post and share like a pro. Download LinkedIn's own sharing tool: https://www.linkedin.com/bookmarklet. This Sharing Bookmarklet allows you to share content from anywhere on the web as an update and as a tweet, a Group discussion, or even as a private message to individuals.

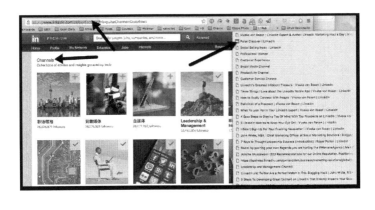

76. USING PULSE FOR CONTENT

LinkedIn Pulse acts as a newsfeed of sorts where you can see Posts from LinkedIn Influencers and search for topics and subjects your connections would be interested in. Save the link in your Favorites. This gives you relevant material to comment on and share with your network.

Either write something worth reading or do something worth writing about.

- Benjamin Franklin

77. POSTS, PUBLISHER, AND PULSE

There is a lot of confusion between Pulse, Posts, and Publisher. They are all related, just different. So here's a simple breakdown:

- Posts are articles you write on LinkedIn
- Publisher is the feature where you write and share your posts.
- Pulse is the newsreader where Influencer and some members' Posts can be seen and read.

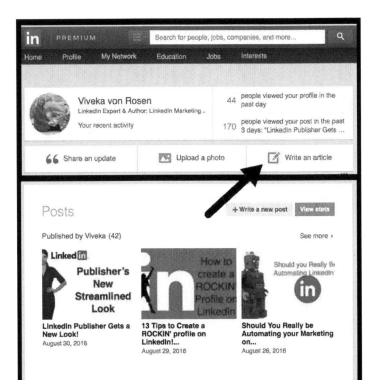

78. WRITE YOUR OWN POSTS

Writing your own posts establishes you as a thought-leader, gets you more visibility, and increases engagement. You can create original posts or even repurpose your more popular blog posts. On the home page, click on "Write an article." Published posts do best when they are over 800 words.

Do or do not; there is no try.

- Yoda

COMPANY PAGES

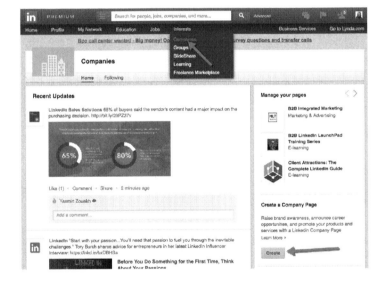

79. CREATING A COMPANY PAGE

According to LinkedIn, over 80% of the 450+ million members want to connect with Company Pages. Create your Company by clicking the Companies link under Interests and on the yellow Create button. Or go to https://www.linkedin.com/company/add/show. You will need a unique website for your email address (name@companyname.com).

80. WORD AGAIN

Start with a Word document as you did before. Copy and paste the About section from your company website as the foundation for your new company page description. Customize it specifically for LinkedIn with an opening message - welcome people to the page and give a brief description of what you offer on this page such as information, promotions, and discounts.

81. KEYWORDS AND FINDABILITY FOR YOUR COMPANY

If relevant, use the same keywords you created for your personal profile in your company page description. You have up to 2000 characters to describe your company. As you did with your personal summary, use white space, special characters, bullets, and capitalization to enhance this description.

82. ADD A COMPANY PAGE IMAGE

This is a real opportunity to create visually arresting images that grab a viewer's attention, and get the visitor to scroll down to your updates. Your image should be 660 x 200 pixels. Create the image yourself with Canva.com or PicMonkey.com, or hire someone to make an image for your LinkedIn page. As mentioned earlier, Fiverr.com is a good source of graphic artists at a reasonable price.

Linked Into Business
Professional Training & Coaching
1-10 employees

1,445 followers   ✓ Following

Home

Follow our
Company Page and
go to
LinkedIntoBusiness.com
for even more tips!

Welcome to our LinkedIn Company Page! I'm glad you found us! At Linked Into Business (LIB) we are here to "MAKE SOCIAL MEDIA WORK FOR YOU"

∨ See more ∨

Recent Updates

Linked Into Business TIP THREE: Linked Into Business Did you know you could customize your LinkedIn Invitations on the Mobile app? Check it out! https://lnkd.in/eKeM2Ae {PS... follow my company page for more great tips like this!}

How to Customize Your Invitations on LinkedIn Mobile...
lnkd.in · {... and other cool LinkedIn Mobile features} Access Your Connections To access your connections, go to the My Network tab to see your contacts' recen

Like · Comment · Share · 2 minutes ago

Linked Into Business TIP TWO: Are you saving your searches yet on LinkedIn? you totally should and here's why! ==>> https://lnkd.in/eWGdZYD

LinkedIn's Saved Search: You MUST Start Using It
linkedin.com · How do you Save a Search on LinkedIn? Recently, Hilde (one of my tribe) asked, "How do you save a search, exactly?" I realized I didn't have a very go

Like · Comment · Share · 2 minutes ago

Linked Into Business TIP ONE: Linked Into Business I usually recommend people turn OFF their Profile Update Notification when making changes on LinkedIn. But here's what happened when I forgot to do it on my own profile!!! Check out my story and see how it can help you amplify your business presence ==>> https://lnkd.in/eeSt3G/

LinkedIn Notifications. A Mistake that Worked Out.
lnkd.in · As one of my connections pointed out, even LinkedIn Experts can make a mistake! This one happened to work out.... I always recommend my clients turn

Like · Comment · Share · 4 minutes ago

How You're Connected

1 first-degree connection
5 second-degree connections
17 Employees on LinkedIn

See all ▸

Linked Into Business Showcase Pages

Linked Into Business
Professional Training...
1-10 employees

LinkedIn Experts
178 followers
✓ Following

LinkedIn Prospecting - Get More Leads!
127 followers

Featured Groups

Linked Strategies
47,014 members
+ Join

Women Speakers...
1,491 members
✓ Member

LinkChat: A group for...
554 members
+ Join

People Also Viewed

power formula

83. COMPANY PAGE UPDATES

An update is similar to a Facebook post or Tweet. Update a few times a week for better visibility. You might consider doing a monthly update series to get people used to going to your company page. Best Of and Top Ten type series work great for this type of update. Add updates each day to build upon the one from the day before.

84. ENCOURAGE ENGAGEMENT ON YOUR COMPANY PAGE

Anyone on LinkedIn can comment on, like, or share a company status update - when they do, their network also sees the post. Share your Company page updates more than once a week on your personal feed as well as encouraging employees to do the same. Send a weekly email to your employees with links to the updates you want shared. You can share to just your employees by choosing "employees only."

85. SPONSORED UPDATES

A sponsored update is when you pay to get your Update seen by more people who are not in your network and do not follow your company page. To get the most bang for your effort, sponsor (pay for) updates that are already doing well. Sponsoring even one or two of the updates will increase the likelihood your posts in the series will be seen, read, and amplified by your growing network of followers.

86. TARGETING YOUR COMPANY PAGE UPDATES

Targeted Company updates can deliver highly relevant content exactly to who you need to be sharing it with which increases engagement. Choose Target Update from the dropdown, and select your targeting criteria including Industry, Seniority, Job Function, Company Size, Non-company Employees, and Geography. You'll need at least 100 people in your targeted criteria for it to work.

87. BRANDING ACROSS YOUR EMPLOYEES' PROFILES

Ask employees to connect their profiles to your Company page. Have employees add or edit their existing Experience section, choosing your company from the dropdown menu to connect to your Company Page. This has the added benefit of creating a navigation link and embedding your logo on their personal profiles. This serves to amplify your Company page.

SOCIAL ENGAGEMENT

"Build it, and they will come" only works in the movies. Social Media is a "build it, nurture it, engage them and they may come and stay."

- Seth Godin, Author and Influencer

88. JOIN STRATEGIC GROUPS

Join LinkedIn groups in your own market or industry, your ideal client's industry, groups you are interested in, groups your target prospects are members of, alumni groups, and/or your own company's group. Once you join a group, you can send messages to strategic members and prospects (up to 15 a month in ALL your groups total) or invite strategic members to connect with you.

It doesn't matter how the paint is put on, as long as something is said.

- Jackson Pollack, Artist, Innovator, and Disruptor

89. CREATE A GROUP

Consider creating a Standard or Unlisted Group on LinkedIn. Task someone in the group or in your company to moderate it in order to keep it interesting and relevant. Make your group a destination by keeping it a current and active forum.

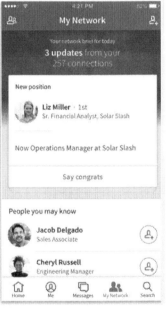

90. BE MOBILE WITH LINKEDIN

Build your brand on the fly using the LinkedIn mobile app. Take a picture that will help build your brand and share it as an update. Regular updates work too. You can edit while on the move. Are you at a conference and realize your profile has your old position listed as your current job? Or there's a blaring spelling error? No problem. You can now edit (most) of your profile from your mobile LinkedIn app.

Marketing is never done. It's about perpetual motion. We must continue to innovate every day.

- Beth Comstock, Author

91. MANAGE AND MAINTAIN YOUR INBOX

Just as you do with your email, keep on top of your LinkedIn inbox in a timely manner. You don't want to miss important connections, messages, and new prospects. By the way, at this writing, the mobile app inbox (LinkedIn Messenger) is actually easier to use than LinkedIn on your desktop or laptop browser.

92. ADD LINKEDIN TO YOUR EMAIL SIGNATURE

A dd your customized LinkedIn link to your email signature. If you have a Company or Group page, add those links as well. A call to action with your signature - *Let's connect on LinkedIn* - works well too. There are many free online tools, such as WiseStamp, that create professional email signatures with embedded social links across most mail services.

93. ADD LINKEDIN TO YOUR WEBSITE

If you have a website, add your LinkedIn customized URL link and/or your Company page link. There are several plugins to choose from that will do it for you. Search LinkedIn Company Page Plugin to get an embed code. Or ask your web developer to add one for you.

94. ADD LINKEDIN TO YOUR BUSINESS CARD

Add your customized LinkedIn link to your business cards. Business card companies (like Vistaprint) have the option of adding your social info and populate it with the appropriate social icon. If you change your customized link in the future, don't forget to change it on your cards.

95. SHARE ACROSS SOCIAL MEDIA PLATFORMS

Share your personal, company, and LinkedIn group links across all your social media sites. Give potential connections a reason why they should connect with you – great information, discounts, important updates, etc. Share those links a few times a month, just to let people know where you are active.

96. SEND A PERSONAL EMAIL
TO YOUR NETWORK

Compose a message to your email list letting them know about your updated LinkedIn profile or your new LinkedIn group and/or Company page. As always, let your network know why they should connect with you or follow your Company page and/or Group. Mention you will be sharing resources, promos, events, and a community they will not be able to find anywhere else.

97. PAID SERVICES

At this writing, you can get access to three main premium LinkedIn accounts; Jobseeker, Business Plus, and Sales Navigator. These give you better search fields, the ability to see everyone who has viewed your profile, and extra InMails. Business Plus gives you more saved searches, better paid search fields, and more InMails.

98. CREATE AN UPDATE SCHEDULE

This is not only true for LinkedIn, but very useful for social media in general. If you create a schedule you are more likely to stick too it. Unless something is urgent or extremely timely, set days and times that work best for you. Keep a file of things you would like to share when it comes time to update on LinkedIn.

Daily Checklist

Home Page (Notifications):
- [ ] Check and Respond to "Viewed my Profile"
- [ ] Check "People You May Know" and add connections
- [ ] Respond to Update comments and shares
- [ ] Respond to Endorsements
- [ ] Comment on a Post

Inbox:
- [ ] Delete Spam from Inbox
- [ ] "Archive" interesting – not important
- [ ] Respond to requests/messages
- [ ] Forward Introductions
- [ ] Accept "unknown" invitations (with pre-written script)
- [ ] Accept "known" invitations (with personal note)
- [ ] Send message to one known person in your contact list
- [ ] Send message to one unknown person in your contact list

Contacts
- [ ] TAG your new connections
- [ ] Make notes on new connections
- [ ] Set up reminders for new connections
- [ ] Respond to Announcements
- [ ] Send a message campaign to a tagged segment

Groups
- [ ] "Like" or comment on discussions in group
- [ ] Post a Discussion
- [ ] Invite 3 group members to connect
- [ ] Send a message to a Prospect

Posting
- [ ] Post updates (2x a day)
- [ ] Post on Publisher (1x a week)

99. CREATE A CHECKLIST

Create a checklist of daily, weekly, monthly and one-time only actions. Daily actions should include reaching out to your best connections and sharing posts as well as responding to messages, people who have viewed your profile or have commented on or shared your posts or updates. Every week you should write a post and connect to new prospects. Every month you should do a quick review of your profile and make sure it's up to date.

100. DELEGATE WHAT YOU CAN

If you are lucky enough to have an assistant, delegate your inbox, invitations, tagging, and messaging campaigns. These are all fundamental to success on LinkedIn. If you don't have an assistant, this might be a good time to start thinking about someone, even if it is for a few hours a week. LinkedIn is an important business tool that needs tending for success.

101. FOLLOW THE GOLDEN RULE

Do unto others as you would have them do unto you. LinkedIn is about connecting and engaging and creating real relationships. Do more than market and advertise all the time. Instead, share valuable information, answer questions, share others' updates, or pass on new job information. Remember, on LinkedIn or anywhere, the more you give, the more you get!

Be yourself. Everyone else is taken.

- Oscar Wilde, Author

FINAL WORDS

by Dayna Steele

As we were working on this book, Microsoft announced the acquisition of LinkedIn. As with any corporate merger, things may change. With that said, the essence of LinkedIn will not change. It is still and will remain a great way to connect with like-minded individuals and potential customers and collaborators all over the world. Looking for a job? Replace the words *clients*, *customers*, and *collaborators* in this book with the word *employers*. Bottom line: LinkedIn is a great way to be found by anyone in business.

With strong social media working knowledge, I thought I had a pretty good profile until I started this project with Viveka. Once the first draft was done, I reviewed the book and my own LinkedIn profile tip by tip. I definitely was not using LinkedIn even close to its full potential. After taking our advice and following the tips in this book, my profile views were up 54% in the first week alone. Since that time, I have connected with future clients on LinkedIn and booked several speaking appearances at conferences and meetings over the next year through these new contacts.

Consistency is key when creating your personal brand. The more consistent you are, the stronger you brand yourself and your abilities. Focus on what you do best and let the world know using the powerful tool that is LinkedIn. I particularly like the first part of our book as it guides you through creating this foundation before you even start filling anything out on LinkedIn. This is personal branding you can then extend to your marketing, website, business cards, brochures, and more. Be consistent across all platforms and watch your brand grow.

As Viveka said in her open, a book does not happen with just an author – it takes a village. Thanks to Viveka for being such a great and willing collaborator and friend. To Colin Gold for taking valuable time to try our tips until we got them just right. To my LinkedIn network who teach me so much every day. To my sons who are often ignored while I'm in the "book writing zone." And, as always, to Charlie the Wonder Husband for being wonderful.

LinkedIn is a great business tool. It is also a social media platform and the point of social media is just that – to be social. To network with others. To collaborate. To share information. Work your way through all 101 tips in this book and watch your network grow!

Dayna Steele is the creator of Your Daily Success Tip and the 101 Ways to Rock Your World book series. As a popular business keynote speaker, she tells success stories based on lessons she learned from working with the world's greatest rock stars. Dayna also wrote Surviving Alzheimer's with Friends, Facebook, and a Really Big Glass of Wine. *In her spare time, she drinks good wine and plays bad golf.*

CONTACT THE AUTHORS

A network is everything to success – it would be an honor to join yours. Connect with us here:

Viveka von Rosen
www.linkedin.com/in/linkedinexpert
viveka@linkedintobusiness.com
www.linkedintobusiness.com
(970) 481-8916

Dayna Steele
www.linkedin.com/in/daynasteele
dayna@daynasteele.com
www.daynasteele.com
(281) 738-3254

Notes:

Notes:

Notes:

Made in the USA
San Bernardino, CA
23 October 2016